# SOLDIERS OF THE LIGHT

## CLAIRE ELIZABETH GROSE

Copyright © 2023 by Claire Elizabeth Grose

Compiled and edited by Michael Grose and June Kennedy

All rights reserved. No portion of this publication may be reproduced, stored in a retrieval system or transmitted in any form by any means – electronic, mechanical, photocopying, recording, or any other –except for brief quotation in printed reviews, without the prior written permission of the publisher.

Unless indicated otherwise, all scripture quotations in this book are from the following source:

The Good News Bible: The Bible in Today's English Version (TEV) © 1976 by the American Bible Society. Used with permission.

ISBN 978-0-6486884-9-5

Author contact information - clairegrose.heartmatters@gmail.com

Version 1.0

# DEDICATION

This book is dedicated to Charles,
a true Soldier of the Light, Prayer Warrior
and longtime friend.

# CONTENTS

| | |
|---|---|
| **DEDICATION** | IV |
| **CONTENTS** | V |
| **PREFACE** | VIII |
| **ACKNOWLEDGEMENTS** | X |
| PART ONE | 1 |
|     MY DAILY PRAYER | 4 |
|     SPREAD YOUR LIGHT | 5 |
|     THE POWER OF HIS WORD | 6 |
|     THE FAINTEST HINT OF SUNRISE | 7 |
|     UNION OF FATHER AND CHILD | 8 |
|     SWEET FRAGRANCE | 9 |
|     SIDE BY SIDE | 10 |
|     SPRINGTIME BLOOMS | 11 |
|     SUNRAYS | 14 |
|     RIGHT HERE, RIGHT NOW | 15 |
|     REFRESH ME LORD | 16 |
|     PRAISE YOUR HOLY NAME | 17 |
|     YOUR LOVE I WANT TO GIVE | 18 |
|     CLOCKWORK | 19 |
|     YOUR BEAUTY IS EVERYWHERE | 20 |
|     I'M LIVING WITH YOU | 21 |
|     EVERY DAWN IS MADE IN HEAVEN | 22 |
|     IN WONDER AND PRAISE | 23 |
|     HIS BEAUTY | 26 |
|     DAWN TO DUSK | 27 |
|     CELEBRATE OUR LOVE | 28 |
|     CHANGING CANOPY | 29 |
| PART TWO | 30 |
|     SOLDIERS OF THE LIGHT | 33 |
|     HOPE IN JESUS | 34 |
|     QUIET TIME WITH GOD | 35 |
|     GOD'S GIFTS | 36 |

| | |
|---|---|
| *YOU LOVE US REGARDLESS* | 37 |
| *TO YOU I BELONG* | 38 |
| *THE YEARS ARE MY LESSONS* | 41 |
| *FAITH IS THE KEY* | 42 |
| *SEARCH LIGHT* | 43 |
| *THE HOURS OF TODAY* | 44 |
| *EVERY HOUR, STEP AND BREATH* | 45 |
| *STEADY AS YOU GO* | 46 |
| *INNER PEACE* | 49 |
| *THANK YOU LORD* | 50 |
| *PROFOUND PEACE* | 51 |
| *DON'T WORRY ABOUT TOMORROW* | 52 |
| *LIVING IN HARMONY* | 53 |
| *FLOOD GATES OF THE HEART* | 54 |
| *COME BACK TO HIS LOVE* | 57 |
| *IN UNISON WITH GOD* | 58 |
| *LET ME LOVE YOU* | 59 |
| *EMBRACE MY SORRY HEART* | 60 |
| *I MATTER TO YOU LORD* | 61 |
| *HIS SUPPLY IS ENDLESS* | 62 |
| *YOU KNOW WHAT I NEED LORD* | 63 |
| *A HIGHER PLACE* | 64 |
| *BIRTH OF TODAY* | 65 |
| *TODAY THERE'S A NEED* | 66 |
| *YOUR HANDS MADE US* | 67 |
| *ARMS OF LIGHT* | 68 |
| PART THREE | 69 |
| *THE LORD'S RADIANCE* | 72 |
| *THE STIRRING OF YOUR SPIRIT LORD* | 73 |
| *BE MY LIGHT AND GUIDE LORD* | 74 |
| *A PLACE IN HIS HOME* | 75 |
| *BELIEVE AND RECEIVE* | 76 |
| *THE SACRED SOUL* | 77 |
| *SHIELD OF FAITH* | 80 |
| *CALL ON THE HOLY SPIRIT* | 81 |

| | |
|---|---|
| FACE TO FACE | 82 |
| HIS GIFT OF LOVE | 83 |
| YOUR SPIRIT LORD | 84 |
| GOD'S DOMAIN | 85 |
| PART FOUR | 86 |
| IN THE SHADOWS OF GETHSEMANE | 89 |
| THE HOLY LAMB | 90 |
| CUP OF SUFFERING | 91 |
| HALLELUJAH IT'S EASTER DAY | 94 |
| KING OF GLORY | 95 |
| CHRISTMAS IS YOU LORD | 98 |
| HEAVENLY ANGELS SING OUT | 99 |
| IMMANUEL, THE LORD | 100 |
| THE SAVIOUR IS BORN | 101 |

# PREFACE

Two things I just wanted to say about this book are, why I started writing and how I came by the title.

I grew up in the 1950's-1960's in Adelaide, South Australia, my life was pretty simple but wonderful. I was very lucky to have a secure family life, and my Mum and Dad brought the family up to treat others with respect, do the right thing, be courteous, and respect your elders. We had a strict upbringing and even as adults our parents never criticized us but encouraged us to do our best in life. They were "Aussie battlers" but we always managed to make it through the tough times!

They were people of integrity and cared about others and instilled that into our family.

Church was a big part of our lives growing up. We went to Sunday School at an early age and progressed up through the appropriate groups as we got older.

Youth groups, camps and church anniversaries were all important to the whole family. We competed in church sports teams, basketball and tennis with other parishes across Adelaide. Life-long friendships were in the making and cherished golden memories to look back on that would never fade.

Bible stories, hymns and choruses were all part of getting to know Jesus. This nurturing finally led me to the day Jesus came knocking on my heart's door. Being filled with the Holy Spirit is something I will never forget and the overwhelming power of His love that filled my whole being and propelled me to the front of the hall to give my heart to Him. No words can fully describe the joy I felt. That was in February 1968, I was 14 years of age. He has been my Shining Light ever since, and lives within me always.

So I thank my beautiful Mum and Dad for the way they raised me and for the foundation of knowing Jesus' love.

It was in His love that I started to write, in the autumn of 1993. My journey has brought me to this book "Soldiers of the Light", because in His Word we are called to pass His message on.

"So stand ready, with truth as a belt tight around your waist, with righteousness as your breastplate, and as your shoes the readiness to announce the Good News of peace. At all times carry faith as a shield; for with it you will be able to put out all the burning arrows shot by the Evil One. And accept salvation as a helmet, and the word of God as the sword which the Spirit gives you."
Ephesians 6:14-17 - Good News Bible.

When I was a young Christian reading my Bible was really important to me in getting to know Jesus as my personal Saviour and became the foundation that I built my faith on.

It gave me strength and courage as I began life in the workforce at the age of 16. Coming from a sheltered upbringing it was my lifeline to self-confidence and adapting to social life at work.
The poems reflect the everyday feelings and emotions that we feel as we meet the challenges of life and how the great magnitude of God's love can help us rise above them.

Many of these writings have been my first words of whispered prayer, so much that I have been moved to write them down at once and continue on in His wonderful and absolute love.

Together we write as He provides my inspiration.

All glory to Him, my precious Lord Jesus!

## ACKNOWLEDGEMENTS

My heartfelt thanks to my beloved family, my Mum and Dad, Lilly and Ken, and my siblings Jeanette, June, Carol, Gloria and Lynne, for their never ending encouragement and support to me. To the rest of the family, you are all a precious link that joins us together.

To Michael and Andrew for your continual support to me in fulfilling my passion of writing poems for the Lord to help others through His Word.

A huge thank you to Junie for editing my poems and the coffees and lunches we enjoyed along the way.

A special big thank you to Joshua Woskett for his magnificent sunset cover photo on the Fleurieu Peninsula, South Australia.

To Joy Furnell for her Crown of Thorns drawing, you have an amazing gift, thank you Joy.

A special thank you to Salisbury Uniting Church, Adelaide for photos, used by permission.

A big thank you to Jane and Scott, Allan, Barry and Lindsay for great photos.

To my friends and Church Families, thank you for your love and support.

To my beautiful sons, Michael and Andrew and your families. Thank you for loving me and I am so glad He gave you to me. I cherish my grandchildren and love you all so much.

To you the reader, thank you for picking this book up and I pray you will find His peace and love on the pages ahead.

May He shower you all with His love and blessings.

# PART ONE

"So stand ready, with truth as a belt tight around your waist, with righteousness as your breastplate, and as your shoes the readiness to announce the Good News of peace. At all times carry faith as a shield; …. And accept salvation as a helmet, and the word of God as the sword which the Spirit gives you."

Ephesians 6 : 14 - 17

# BEHOLD THE LORD…
# WILL LEAD YOU…

"…And so I walk in the presence of God,
in the light that shines on the living."

Psalm 56 : 13

# MY DAILY PRAYER

Be with me, stay with me,
Close by my side,
Fill me with Your peace and love,
So my spirit shall surely fly
To the heights in Your love,
As only You can give,
Prepare me for this day ahead,
So in me You'll always live.

# SPREAD YOUR LIGHT

Your purpose for me Lord
Has finally come to mind,
My true mission I found
To truly spread Your light.

You've laid this on my heart,
I feel with such intent,
A heartfelt purpose to help
Those to me You send.

These words that fall
So tenderly in Your light,
Your desire is for all
To receive the Crown of Life.

Your purpose for me Lord
Is to love so endlessly,
To ease the hunger for peace
That comes with Your grace and mercy.

Yes, Your purpose for me Lord
Is to spread Your light through words
That come from Eternity,
Truly You, I want to serve.

# THE POWER OF HIS WORD

Some power for your heart
You will find in God's Word,
A line or a verse
Will make your heart yearn.

We all need reassurance
To surge through life,
A few moments of your time
Will make things come right.

Reach for His Word
And a blessing you will find,
A verse will speak to you
At the right time!

Just the power of His Word
Are moments through your day,
The perfect lift you need
To send you on your way.

His love will dispel
Those anxious moments ahead,
The power of His Word
Will give you peace and strength.

# THE FAINTEST HINT OF SUNRISE

The faintest hint of sunrise Lord,
That's Mother Earth coming to life,
The puffy clouds reflect
Dawn's colours in the light.

The faintest hint of sunrise Lord,
The dew melts away
With steamy shrouds that rise
To the Heavens on their way.

The faintest hint of sunrise Lord
As Winter fog lays low,
As sunrise breaks the horizon
Her beams begin to show.

The faintest hint of sunrise Lord,
Your salvation for the day
Be with us each hour
As we journey on our way.

Yes, the faintest hint of sunrise Lord,
Marks a brand new day,
My special time to find You
Before the hours roll away.

# UNION OF FATHER AND CHILD

The union of Father and child
Is the calling of God's Spirit,
To all who answer His call
Whenever they may hear it.

The sweet union with the Divine,
So special within your soul,
It will stir the depths of your heart
And completely make you whole.

This union of Father and child,
Unique only to the realms of Heaven,
A blessing from the Saviour
That stays with you forever.

A baptism of pure love,
Anointed with Holy oil,
A balm so complete
Will ordain you as His child.

The union of Father and child,
There's nothing more you need,
He is the King of Heaven
And you His Holy seed.

# SWEET FRAGRANCE

Smell that sweet fragrance
In gardens everywhere,
The aroma of Christ
To lift you from your cares.

His sweet fragrance will restore you
And His balm will heal your hurts,
Memories will fade away
That made you sad at first!

Perfumes in flowers
And colours so divine,
His sweet fragrance will thrill you
And make your heart shine.

So claim His sweet fragrance
To anoint your daily path,
Drift through His aroma
That will bring you to His arms.

## SIDE BY SIDE

You are my life line
When I'm weak or strong,
When I'm happy or sad
Side by side we belong.

You are my life line
Whether I'm young or old,
To You it makes no difference
As long as I'm one of Your fold.

You are my life line
You supply my needs,
That You already know
Before I ask for these!

You are my life line,
Side by side we'll always stay,
Your power and Your glory
Will surround me day by day.

Yes, side by side we belong
For all eternity,
In spirit and in truth
I will see Your victory.

## SPRINGTIME BLOOMS

Springtime blooms,
New life erupts,
From new born buds,
They bring their love.

Springtime blooms,
A fragrance so sweet,
From the Lord Himself,
Aromas to meet.

His beauty in form to rise,
Awakes from sleep to tantalize!
A thrill so tender for the soul
Will lift the hearts of young and old.

Yes, Springtime blooms
A must to seek,
God's glory on show
Sweet joy you will meet.

# GOD IS THE...
# COMMANDER OF THE WORD...

"But thanks be to God who gives us the
victory through our Lord Jesus Christ!"

1 Corinthians 15 : 57

# SUNRAYS

Sunrays touch my heart each day
With joy in earthly splendour,
No words can describe
This early morning wonder.

Heaven's perfect beams of light
Spilling from lofty clouds,
Reaching for the horizon,
Such delight my soul has found.

The hazy beams bring wonder,
So proudly they display
Sunrays in such glory
That herald every day.

Sunrays seem to soothe and calm,
They follow dawn's awaking,
Food for my soul,
A new day in the making!

# RIGHT HERE, RIGHT NOW

I feel Your Spirit with me
With rays that reach my soul,
So tenderly they soothe me,
They make me feel whole.

Right here, right now,
Your light so warm and bright
Touches my heart
And makes everything alright!

Right here, right now
I feel contentment flow,
A peace and calm so real,
From God above I know.

Right here, right now,
My doubts just fade away,
My faith in Him so strong,
I trust Him today.

Right here, right now,
His presence so profound,
My faith and trust stands firm,
My feet on solid ground.

# REFRESH ME LORD

Refresh me Lord
In the early morn,
As the dampness is felt
And the new dawn is born.

Refresh me Lord
As my day begins,
Help me to be mindful
That You live within.

Refresh me Lord
Lift me up through the day,
Keep my thoughts in a safe place
Where they cannot stray.

Refresh me Lord
In Your wisdom and strength,
To face the day in Your grace,
That's where I begin.

I must step into Your footprint
As I navigate my day,
So refresh me Lord
As I go on my way.

# PRAISE YOUR HOLY NAME

I praise Your Holy Name Lord,
Blessed is Your name,
You thrill my heart and soul,
You will never change!

You are my Holy Saviour,
My omnipotent, glorious King,
You live forever
You are the King of Kings!

You sit at the right hand of God,
I praise Your Holy Name,
In Heaven upon Your Throne,
Forever You are the same.

I praise Your Holy Name Lord,
You rule over Heaven and Earth,
Sacred You are,
You will always be the first!

# YOUR LOVE I WANT TO GIVE

Thank You Lord
That I live with You,
So each day of my life
You help me through.

You called me many years ago
When Your Spirit came to live
With me in all Your fullness,
Now Your love I want to give.

I write from Your prompting
In praise and worship for You,
To pen Your words of love
Because I truly want to.

Your love I want to give
Through inspiration I receive,
To write in verse
So Your beloved will believe.

# CLOCKWORK

It's break of day,
Sun meets the horizon,
Night rolls over
As daylight comes to life.

The stars in heaven now dim,
The sun outshines their light,
The moon now on the other side,
Lighting up the night.

Everything has a plan Lord
Designed by You,
Your perfect clockwork
That only You can do.

Precious Lord these wonders,
One day you'll tell us how
They all came to be,
What we see right now.

The earth turns like clockwork,
No man could instigate,
Only the hand of God
These wonders could create!

# YOUR BEAUTY IS EVERYWHERE

You spoil me Lord with Your beauty,
Your Sun and Your Moon,
A never ending glory
Like the Spring and Summer blooms.

My adoration flies
To the heights in Your love,
Blessing my every footstep
You give me from above.

Your beauty is everywhere Lord,
I see it every day,
A never ending blessing
That sends me on my way.

Your beauty is everywhere Lord
For our delight,
The wonders of this world
Seem to make things right!

# I'M LIVING WITH YOU

Lord, I'm living with you
In my heart and soul,
Daily I need You
To make me whole.

I am complete in Your love
Because You lead me on,
To victory every day,
My faith makes me strong.

Our love is forever
You supply all I need,
Now that You live within
Your blessings I receive.

My heart overflows
Where Your Spirit lives,
Nothing in this world
Can ever compete.

I'm living with You Lord,
Every day of my life,
Thank you Lord Jesus
You are my shining light.

# EVERY DAWN IS MADE IN HEAVEN

The sprinkling of dawn across the sky,
I see light waking up,
The stars begin to fade
As sun appears soon enough.

Memories of yesterday dim,
My Lord is by my side,
Reality stirs within the heart
But Your presence comes to mind.

I whisper a thankful prayer
That dawn has now arrived,
Your colours surely a sign
You made this sunrise.

Every dawn is made in Heaven,
Each one so unique,
Your hand is surely in it,
As today Your will I seek.

## IN WONDER AND PRAISE

In wonder and praise I find You Lord,
I open my heart to you,
Matters within I can't dispel,
I can only hand them to You.

In wonder and praise I love You Lord,
My companion every day,
I search Your Words for solace
Which helps me find my way.

Your Word is ever true
As I find confirmation of Your love,
In wonder and praise I'm renewed
Because I seek Your guidance from above.

In wonder and praise I bow to You Lord,
My Eternal Almighty Lord,
You gave me the Holy Spirit,
Now it's You, it's You I adore.

# COMMIT YOUR…
# ALLEGIANCE TO GOD…

"The Lord is our protector and glorious king, blessing us with kindness and honour…"

Psalm 84 : 11

# HIS BEAUTY

His beauty is forever
And shines on all the world,
It is all around us,
Daily it unfurls.

It reaches all corners of the earth,
No matter how far or wide,
His beauty is around us
For every searching eye.

His beauty found in simple things
Like a dried autumn leaf,
Or the reflection in a puddle
Of a bird stretching its wings.

His beauty holds such grandeur
As an icy mountain peak,
Or in a green sheltered valley
Providing shade from the heat.

His true beauty is His Light
That will never fade,
A radiance unspeakable
When you meet Him on that day!

## DAWN TO DUSK

Dawn sweeps the horizon
In shades of grey and mauve,
Rising sun delivers
Golden sunbursts that explode.

The sea; like glass reflects
Her brilliance to the eye,
Like a shining mirror
Such beauty from the sky.

Solace comes to meet
The heart and soul that feels,
The effects of glorious dawn
Makes me want to kneel!

Your beauty Lord so amazing
Give You praise I must,
Thank You for sweeping dawn
As she makes her way to dusk!

## CELEBRATE OUR LOVE

Let's celebrate our love Lord,
So precious from You alone,
Though my heart feels bruised,
I seek refuge at Your Throne.

I celebrate our love Lord,
Because Your love for me You've shown,
You found me and took me in,
You made my heart Your home.

I celebrate our love Lord,
None other will do,
You paid a heavy price
That I will never owe to You.

So let's celebrate our love Lord
That belongs in Eternity,
Your gift beyond words,
That brings me to my knees.

# CHANGING CANOPY

I look to the heavens above my head,
Changing scenes I see,
Clouds in a rush sometimes,
Still bring wonder to me.

Clouds, blue skies and stars
All a changing canopy,
An ever evolving scene
Brings You close to me!

Thank You Lord for Mother Nature,
Though sometimes she's wild and rough,
Her beauty is so awesome,
Acknowledge You; we must.

All neatly set and positioned
Earth spins in space,
The Globe's ever changing canopy,
In a moment changes take place.

# PART TWO

"The Lord is my protector; he is my strong fortress.
My God is my protection, and with him I am safe.
He protects me like a shield; he defends me
and keeps me safe. He is my Saviour;
he protects me and saves me from violence."

2 Samuel 22 : 2 - 3

# STAND FIRM...
# IN YOUR FAITH...

"Give me again the joy that comes from your salvation, and make me willing to obey you."

Psalm 51 : 12

# SOLDIERS OF THE LIGHT

We struggle to fight morality
And the pressure that lays within,
But Jesus calls for peace,
Only He was without sin.

We can win this battle many times
With Jesus Christ our Lord,
With His shield of Mercy
We can beat this raging war.

His strategy lies in kindness
And to keep a level head,
With a gaze that's set on heaven
We can leave fear in its dread.

Christ won the battle of Calvary,
He rose victorious for eternal life,
He conquered the battle of sin
So we could be soldiers of the light.

As soldiers of the light,
We carry His Orb of Peace,
And wear His armour of love
For all we are yet to meet.

# HOPE IN JESUS

In those moments when you feel weak,
You lose sight of hope in your sorrow,
Reach for His Holy Word
Another dawn will rise tomorrow.

Stop for a moment
And call the Lord to your side,
Ask Him to take the pain,
On Him you can rely.

Look to hope in Jesus,
Forever He will hold you tight,
Forgive yourself of the past,
Live tomorrow in His light.

Leave regrets behind you,
Hold onto hope in Jesus right now,
Exchange grief for happiness today,
The Saviour will show you how.

Listen to the voice in your heart
And keep hope in Jesus today,
Take that step in faith,
You need not be afraid.

# QUIET TIME WITH GOD

Quiet time with God
Aligns every kind of heart,
Bear your cares to the Saviour,
He will take you into His arms.

Confess your deepest cares,
Offer up your wounds and hurts,
Quiet time with the King of Kings,
Every word is heard.

He will come with His balm to soothe you,
Just wait in silence to be healed,
Whisper the words "I receive",
His Holy Spirit will be revealed.

So quiet time with God,
No other treasure will do,
You will soar to the heights in His love,
His Holy Spirit will live on in you!

## GOD'S GIFTS

God's gifts He freely gives
To every person on earth,
Love, grace, peace and mercy,
But love was the first.

He made us in His image,
What a privilege to bear,
He bestowed us with talents
So those we could share.

Claim His reassurance and peace
Every day of your life,
He will deliver in full
So you can walk in His light.

God's gifts of grace and mercy,
His pardon to forgive our sin,
He sees into your heart
Where His Holy Spirit lives.

To all who believe in Him
Will receive eternal life,
We then will live in His presence
And receive the Crown of Life.

## YOU LOVE US REGARDLESS

You love us Lord, regardless
Of who we are or what we've done,
You are the Holy Messiah,
God's own precious Son.

You remained without sin
While You were here with us,
You taught us how to love
And be Your daughters and sons.

You love us regardless,
Your forgiveness beyond our belief,
We will never understand
Your love beyond our dreams.

You've prepared Eternity
For all who love You so,
Because You love regardless,
A crown from You we'll own.

# TO YOU I BELONG

When I'm weak
You make me strong,
You call me to Your side
Where I belong.

When I'm sad
You cheer me up,
When I ask for Your help
I receive Your love.

When I feel lonely
I call to You,
There is no other
Who can lift my blues.

Life will give me challenges
But in You I am strong,
Together we work them out
Because to You I belong.

## THE SPIRIT WILL BE YOUR GUIDE...
## TO EVERY CHALLENGE IN LIFE...

"The God who said, "Out of darkness the light shall shine!" is
the same God who made his light shine in our hearts,
to bring us the knowledge of God's glory shining in the
face of Christ."

2 Corinthians 4 : 6

# THE YEARS ARE MY LESSONS

It doesn't matter in this world
What passes me,
When I focus on You Lord,
The One I see.

It doesn't matter in this world
What ills I feel,
My Lord and my Master
For You, I kneel.

Words still hurt me
But my soul inside,
Holds a love so strong
For my Saviour; my guide.

The journey is steep
By Your standards alone,
The years are my lessons
As I travel this road.

One day when we meet
I shall kiss Your feet,
I'll bow before You Lord
At Your Holy seat.

# FAITH IS THE KEY

Pure joy profound
Fills my heart and soul,
A moment's peace from Heaven
Surely must be told.

I know it was my Saviour
Shining through my heart,
A love full of rapture,
The Holy Spirit's mark!

Faith is the key
To Heaven's delights,
His grace and mercy
Will make you shine so bright.

You can overcome
Cares in your life,
Faith is the key
To a happy, balanced life.

# SEARCH LIGHT

A lighthouse in a storm
Is a refuge indeed,
To guide you safely through
To a safe place in need.

Jesus is your search light,
Forever guiding you
Through the storms of life
If you ask Him to.

He will help you bear
The weight as you cling
To His open arms,
The precious King of Kings.

He will guide you to safety,
To a brighter place,
His search light will find you,
Make no mistake.

His search light a beacon
For every challenge of life,
An assurance every day
That Jesus you can find.

# THE HOURS OF TODAY

Walking through the hours of today
Help is at hand,
Jesus is closer than you think,
He truly understands.

He wants to celebrate your joys
And lift you out of your sorrows,
When you share with Him
All of your tomorrows.

Walking through the hours of today
Whether slow or fast,
The Saviour will gently guide you,
You only have to ask.

He craves to be your guide
In all that you do,
Simply ask Him for help,
Your path He will walk with you.

Walking through the hours of today,
An arduous task it need not be,
Look to the Saviour for comfort,
He will supply your every need.

# EVERY HOUR, STEP AND BREATH

Every hour, step and breath Lord
You desire our faithfulness,
To spend time with You
So we can be our best!

Though morality takes its toll,
We can be powered in Your love,
The challenges we face together,
In You we can overcome.

You adore me to the core Lord,
In every hour, step and breath,
You will supply my every need
If I look to You for rest.

So thank You for Your devotion Lord
As is recorded in Your Word,
In our every hour, step and breath,
You are there at every turn.

## STEADY AS YOU GO

Lord, thank You for Your love,
That's with me day and night,
Steady as I go,
I feel You by my side.

Thank You for Your guiding hand,
A Father to His child,
You attend to every need
With a heavenly smile.

Thank You for Your Holy Spirit,
My Comforter and Shield,
Showing me Your love
So pure and real.

Thank You for Your light Lord,
That shines so endlessly,
On Your beloved Lord,
Who You love so tenderly.

Yes, I'm steady as I go Lord
All because of You,
Keep me in Your peace and calm
My whole life through.

## PUT YOUR TRUST AND FAITH...
## IN THE SAVIOUR...

"Remember that I have commanded you to be determined and confident! Do not be afraid or discouraged, for I, the Lord your God, am with you wherever you go."

Joshua 1 : 9

# INNER PEACE

Inner peace is what came to me
As I lay waking up,
While the shadows disappeared
The dawn came soon enough.

I felt content with my life
In that moment of time,
I knew God was looking after me,
He lives in this heart of mine.

Inner peace so vital
For a calm and soothing life,
Against the daily torrents
That sometimes seems so rife.

For that moment of inner peace,
My thoughts were hushed and still,
I was enjoying the release
Of the Holy Spirit's will.

I crave inner peace
For all people of the world,
So we can live in harmony
With Christ Jesus at the helm!

# THANK YOU LORD

Thank You for Your love Lord
That spills over me,
It washes away trapped hurts
And heals the scars I see.

Like soothing oil
It coats and seals
The wounds that still weep
So Your love can be revealed.

Only You understand
The way that I feel,
My trust and faith in You Lord
Will surely make them heal.

So thank You Lord for Your love
That You give abundantly
To every precious soul
Who You name Your family.

# PROFOUND PEACE

Profound peace came to me,
It was laid upon my heart,
A great comfort I felt
As my day was about to start.

I didn't know why I felt like this,
I sensed "peace" was with me,
So profound and complete
I wondered "how could this be"?

As I was driving home from work,
Thick smoke billowed ahead,
I could see the road was closed,
The unknown I started to dread.

A fire was raging in the distance,
So I had to drive the long way round,
Dear family worried for my safety
Until I was safe and sound.

That profound peace I felt,
I will never forget
How real the Holy Spirit is,
He cares, He loves, He protects.

He knew the fire was coming,
He was telling me not to fear,
He is our great comforter and shield,
I know Him, I love Him; so dear.

## DON'T WORRY ABOUT TOMORROW

Don't worry about tomorrow
Get through today,
The hours to come
Will pave the way.

Don't worry about tomorrow
The Lord has it in control,
A test of faith is required
As He moves in your soul.

Don't worry about tomorrow
It has already been planned,
Look at today,
Take hold of His hand.

Though your heart be in turmoil,
You can't think of anything else,
Just for a moment take a step back,
Turn to Jesus not to self.

So don't worry about tomorrow
It will take care of itself,
Look to the Saviour above,
Claim His peace, calm and help.

# LIVING IN HARMONY

To get the best out of life
Harmony is the key,
Jesus came to save us,
Only in Him can this be.

For He is love itself,
He is God incarnate alone,
He sits at the right hand of God,
Upon His heavenly Throne.

Only He sees each heart
And what lies within,
He takes account of acts of kindness,
He doesn't count our sin.

He commands that we love each other
And ask in His Name
For His forgiveness and grace,
For this to earth He came.

His gift is Eternity
To every believing heart,
We are His beloved,
Faith and trust is where you start.

# FLOOD GATES OF THE HEART

When I visit God's House,
A place of strength and divinity,
I feel my soul open
To reveal what lies beneath.

Many wounds still weep
And some scars are rough,
Vulnerability is raw
So I come to His House in trust.

My heart tells me
Tear drops want to fall,
It murmurs "in my weakness
To You I call".

It comes without knowing,
I had no plan to share,
What my soul exposed
To Jesus waiting there.

Nothing could stop the flood gates
Flung open wide,
As my heart-break continued
While my tears ran from inside!

There's no other place to be
When the unexpected strikes a chord,
But to be in God's House
When Jesus comes to call.

# SEEK THE FORTRESS OF GOD…

"You bless those who obey you, Lord;
your love protects them like a shield."

Psalm 5 : 12

## COME BACK TO HIS LOVE

Come back to His love
When distractions call you away,
When the rush is over
Your thoughts can have their say!

The Saviour silently waits
For your whispered prayer,
Silence the voices inside
So you can share your desires there.

Come back to His love
A fountain of endless care,
He never leaves you,
So share some time in prayer.

Give up your earthly banter,
Think thoughts of heaven's delights,
His angels are all around you
Who come from Heaven's skies.

Come back to His love for peace,
Where your fears have no place,
His joys you will truly know
As you look upon His face.

# IN UNISON WITH GOD

There comes a time in your life
When distractions fade,
There seems only one life line
That always stays the same.

When you live in unison with God,
He knows your doubts and cares,
He will never leave you,
Your concerns He'll gladly bear.

Walking in unison with God,
He supplies His mercy and grace,
His gift to all who believe
In Him with trust and faith.

Walk in unison with God
Your eternal companion for life,
He will anoint you as His child,
Because you are precious in His sight.

## LET ME LOVE YOU

Let me love You Lord,
Lover of my soul,
As my faith grows deeper,
You continue to make me whole.

Let me love You Lord,
With a love that knows no end,
Eternal love from You
That Your Spirit sends.

Let me love You Lord
With child-like trust,
Believing without question,
That You are the Son of God.

Yes, let me love You Lord
Into Eternity,
With a love that knows no bounds,
In the Holy Trinity.

# EMBRACE MY SORRY HEART

Embrace my sorry heart Lord
In the realms of Your light,
So it can recover and rebuild
Because I'm precious in Your sight.

Make the chains fall away
With Your grace that is free,
So I can forgive myself
To live the life You planned for me.

Embrace my sorry heart Lord
In Your mercy and strength,
So it can smile again
And try to make amends.

Embrace my hopeful heart Lord
Held in Your pierced hands,
So healing can begin
To carry out Your plans.

# I MATTER TO YOU LORD

I matter to You Lord,
My King, Confidante and Guide,
My Counsellor ever waiting
From You I cannot hide!

You love me endlessly Lord,
All day You crave my love,
My offering of all things
I've learnt to share with You above.

It matters to You Lord
The state of mind I'm in,
Happy or sad You want me
To confess what lies within.

You want the best for me Lord,
I only have to believe
That You are my Risen Lord,
So I bow on bended knee.

Yes I matter to You Lord,
All my days You have allowed,
You planned them long ago Lord,
Your Redemption I have found.

## HIS SUPPLY IS ENDLESS

The Lord's supply is endless
When your heart trusts in Him,
Calling on your faith and hope,
He will fill it to the brim.

For strength and reassurance
Be sure it will come,
In His peace and calm
The battle will be won.

His supply is endless
For cares that persist,
Take them to the Saviour,
He's waiting to assist!

His supply is endless
With a faith so true,
Christ Jesus will help you
Because He truly loves you.

# YOU KNOW WHAT I NEED LORD

You know what I need Lord
Above my selfishness,
I know what I want
But in You I can be my best.

I know I have failed You
In the years gone by,
But my spiritual walk has grown,
And my faith has taken flight.

You know what I need Lord,
Though my wants overflow,
My heart tells me otherwise,
By Your lessons to me You've shown.

I still need reminders
To walk in Your light,
You know what I need Lord
To make things right.

Your path of righteousness
Is narrow and high,
But You know what I need Lord
In my journey of life to survive.

# A HIGHER PLACE

My heart can rise to a higher place
When I focus on my Lord,
Though it may be trembling
From tears I can't ignore.

My thoughts can justify
Moving to a higher place,
Flooded in Your light Lord
I can call on Your mercy and grace.

Past actions in my life
Still cause me some regret,
But if I look to Your higher place
These I can forget!

You are the King of Kings
Who abides in a higher place,
At the Right Hand of God
Our intercession You make.

When doubts and fears come calling,
Take them to a higher place,
His Throne of Gold is waiting
To replace them with His grace.

# BIRTH OF TODAY

As another day is born
Filled with twists and turns,
Look to the Saviour
For you His heart yearns.

The birth of today,
Refreshing to the senses,
We can move forward from the past
From yesterday's lessons.

We can rise above
Shadows that fall,
Ask the Saviour to help you,
He always hears your call.

With time on our side,
Make the most of today,
Walk with faith in your heart,
Don't be afraid!

The Lord calls the dawn,
Each one so unique,
With the birth of today,
His shelter you can seek!

# TODAY THERE'S A NEED

Today, there's a need,
Somebody needs a listening ear,
To spill their heart's concerns
That are shadowed by fear.

Today there's a need
For a helping hand,
Every hour that passes
From a crisis they can't understand.

Today there's a need
Just for a smile or a wave,
A small acknowledgement
Can go a long way.

Today there's a need
To show God's shining light,
A beacon that rescues
Because you are precious in His sight.

Today there's a need
To show the love of Christ,
A tiny seed planted
Will grow to heavenly heights!

## YOUR HANDS MADE US

You made us in Your image Lord,
You hold us in Your hands,
Before we were born,
You made our life-long plans.

More than two thousand years You created,
Sons and daughters of the King,
Your gift of grace and mercy
Is for all who will believe.

Forgive us when we fail
To abide by Your commands,
I crave Your gift of mercy
To retrieve us into Your arms.

So though Your hands made us
And Your Spirit calls us to come,
In time I pray that all
Will worship You the Son.

# ARMS OF LIGHT

His arms of light are there for you
Anytime and any hour,
A beacon to guide you
When you need His power.

He calls for calm,
Compassion and peace,
As a child of God
These gifts you will need.

His arms of light will thrill you so,
A haven for any storm
To guide you to safety,
When you're feeling weary and worn.

Give Jesus your cares
And the weight of life,
He will carry them all
In His arms of light.

His arms of light
Are for all who will come
To be by His side,
God's glorious Son.

# PART THREE

"But thanks be to God who gives us the victory through our Lord Jesus Christ!"

1 Corinthians 15 : 57

# LORD YOU ARE …
# THE SUPREME COMMANDER…

"…More powerful than all armies is he;
he rules supreme."

Psalm 47 : 9

# THE LORD'S RADIANCE

Lord, Your radiance is so bright
Only spirit eyes can see
Your glory in great magnitude,
I can only imagine Thee.

Your radiance so powerful
With a million beams,
Filled with rainbow prisms
Is what I conceive to be.

You are the Almighty,
Everlasting God of Heaven and Earth,
Your radiance shines forever
In Your Kingdom that was the first.

Your radiance so healing,
More than a hundred suns,
Your warmth and balm will soothe
The generations to come.

Yes, Your radiance precious Jesus,
Son of the Holy Trinity,
We can live in Your glory,
We only have to "believe"!

# THE STIRRING OF YOUR SPIRIT LORD

The stirring of Your Spirit Lord
So deep within,
To bring a love overwhelming
That fills me to the brim.

I can't see Him coming
But I feel Him in my heart,
A joy unspeakable
Surely leaves its mark.

At first I don't understand
Why my heart thumps in my chest,
But that's Your Spirit calling me,
He wants me to say "yes"!

The stirring of Your Spirit Lord
Confirms Your love for me,
The foundation of my faith
That's why I love "Thee".

# BE MY LIGHT AND GUIDE LORD

Be my light,
Be my guide,
Be my constant companion
Both day and night.

I need You beside me
As my great comforter and shield,
Prompt me always
To fulfil Thy will.

Be my light and guide Lord
In all I do,
I can't live without You
You are my Saviour, it's true.

You are my light and guide Lord,
You will never let me go,
I praise and worship You Lord,
I love You so.

# A PLACE IN HIS HOME

His mercy seat is waiting
For you to kneel upon;
His Throne of Light is shining
As a beacon to lead you on.

His pierced hand is ready
To hold your own,
His gift of grace will pardon
Your sin from long ago!

A crown is being held
For you to claim and own,
He craves your open heart
So you can have a place in His home.

A divine ear is listening
To every whispered prayer,
His loving arms are opened
To welcome you there!

His Kingdom all prepared
For those who love Him so,
His royal Throne lies waiting
To welcome you home!

# BELIEVE AND RECEIVE

Believe and receive
The King of Glory's love,
Full and overflowing
His blessings will come.

Believe and receive
His blessings will rise,
Joy untold is yours
With every new sunrise.

Believe and receive
His light will make you shine,
His glories will overflow
In this heart of mine.

Believe and receive
Your crown of life,
In His grace and mercy
He will be your guiding light.

Believe and receive
A joy beyond compare,
A knowing in your heart
That Jesus lives there.

## THE SACRED SOUL

The sacred soul so secret,
Your connection to the Lord,
Commit your life to Him
Because it's you He adores.

The world cannot spoil it
Or tarnish its core,
Where the Holy Spirit dwells
To love you more and more.

He will show you God's ways,
But most of all His love
That He showers all over you,
So His Disciple you will become.

A cleansing so pure
Will possess your soul,
You will shine on the inside,
That will make you whole.

The never failing love of Christ
Will never let you go,
His rewards will be many
Because His love you will show!

# YOU ARE THE HIGH PRIEST...
# OF GLORY...

"Your rule is eternal, and you are king forever..."

Psalm 145 : 13

# SHIELD OF FAITH

A vital companion to life
Is a shield of faith,
Your guide and protector
For everything you face.

Faith gives you confidence
And equips you for the fight,
There are battles up ahead
With no warning signs.

The shield of faith is wealth
You can never buy,
It's God's reward
Because you walk in His light.

Answers you will find
With the shield of faith,
A knowing in your soul,
The Spirit's Holy place.

The shield will reflect
The Glory of the Lord,
His light will shine on you
Because it's you He adores.

Gifts He will bestow on you,
Rewards by the score,
When you wear His shield of faith
Because He couldn't love you more.

# CALL ON THE HOLY SPIRIT

Call on the Holy Spirit
To ignite your faith in God,
A never ending presence
For you to lean upon.

Christ gave Him to you
To never leave your side,
Your Comforter and Healer,
With you He will abide.

He brings Christ's warmth and power
To move the soul within,
A heart beat forever
Will live because of Him.

Call on the Holy Spirit,
His power will remain
A blinding torch within you,
You will never be the same.

You can never hide
The manifestation of His love,
This precious gift from God,
Is the power of His love.

# FACE TO FACE

Face to face with Jesus,
His beloved will see
That nothing else compares
In His Eternity.

Face to face with Jesus,
Such pure ecstasy,
A joy unspeakable
Will bring you to your knees.

Face to face with Jesus
You will know rhapsody,
His eyes will hold your gaze,
No tears to run free!

Face to face with Jesus
As cleansing takes place,
Your heart will confess
Choices that were mistakes.

Face to face with Jesus
As you behold the risen King,
You will see His power and glory
When you meet in Eternity!

## HIS GIFT OF LOVE

Thank You Lord, for Your gift of love,
A love that lasts all time,
You my precious Saviour
Every day Your love I find.

You are always there
Regardless of my space,
My distractions may be many
But I still long for Your embrace!

Your gift of love is for all
The nations of the world,
We are Your sons and daughters,
Your Cross was upheld.

Your gift of love is endless,
It will last into Eternity,
No matter who we are
We only have to "believe".

## YOUR SPIRIT LORD

Your Spirit brings a love so real,
Earthly cares fall from place,
Nothing else seems to matter
As we blossom in our faith.

Your Spirit comes quietly Lord,
To bless and bring Your love,
A joy unspeakable
To each receiving heart.

Your Spirit speaks at anytime
To bring all to faith,
So the heart will open
To receive God's Holy grace.

Yes, the faithfulness of Your Spirit Lord
Burns a raging path,
That is so life changing
When we take the time to "ask"!

# GOD'S DOMAIN

The joy of Heaven erupts
When millions of voices sing
Praises to the Holy One,
Glory to Him they bring.

The joy of Heaven so profound;
Nothing can steal it away,
Music so divine to the soul
Is heard in God's domain.

The joy of Heaven waits,
No words can explain,
The ecstasy and wonder
That beholds in God's domain.

The Holy One Himself
Has made this home for us,
Where there is no earthly pain
Only pure joy in Jesus' love.

Yes, God's domain is perfect,
Earth just can't compare,
You will see Him in His glory
When you meet Him there!

## PART FOUR

"'For there is one God, and there is one who brings God and mankind together, the man Christ Jesus, who gave himself to redeem all mankind…"

1 Timothy 2 : 5 - 6

# HE GAVE HIMSELF…
## SO WE COULD HAVE ETERNAL LIFE…

"But Jesus said, "Judas is it with a kiss
that you betray the Son of Man?"

Luke 22 : 48

# IN THE SHADOWS OF GETHSEMANE

Passover dawn awakes,
A promise from long ago,
A prophecy fulfilled,
To Gethsemane the Saviour will go.

A betrayal on the horizon
Had no reprieve,
Set now in motion
In the shadows of Gethsemane.

Bewilderment unleashed
On the chosen few,
How can this be?
Only the Saviour knew.

In the shadows of Gethsemane
Soldiers came to bind
The one so precious,
No sin in Him to find.

His beloved now scattered,
Feared for their lives,
One life for many
Gave the gift of eternal life.

In the shadows of Gethsemane
In the dark of night,
The Lamb of God gave
For you and me, His life.

# THE HOLY LAMB

The sin of the world so great
Only God can hold,
He sent His Son; The Holy Lamb,
In the scriptures we are told.

One life for many
The world would see
He was lifted up
On a Cross at Calvary.

A weight only God can hold
To cancel the debt of man,
Pain we could not imagine,
He endured, the Son of Man.

His heart still loved us
From the arms of the Cross,
His Sacrifice now given
From a promise that was.

The Holy Lamb; God's Beloved Son
Gave His life for you and me,
All so we could have
Eternal life with Him in Eternity.

## CUP OF SUFFERING

Right from His birth
One purpose remained,
The Lord would save us
By His Holy Name.

He would have to bear
The sin of all mankind,
He would die on a Cross,
Centuries before prophesied.

His cup of suffering
Would change the world,
We can live forever,
God sent Him to be upheld.

His message of love
Is for everyone,
He gave His life
So in Him we can be One.

His cup of suffering
Changed the world,
Through His Resurrection we live,
In His hands we are held.

# HALLELUJAH!...
# IT'S EASTER DAY...

"The angel spoke to the women…Come here and see
the place where he was lying.  Go quickly, now,
and tell his disciples, "He has been raised from death  …"

Matthew 28 : 5, 6, 7

# HALLELUJAH IT'S EASTER DAY

As promised in His Word,
The Lamb would rise to life
On the Third Day,
Borne from God; Eternal Life.

His Kingdom now to build
For those who will believe
That He died on the Cross,
Now He lives, victory!

Hallelujah it's Easter Day,
The soul of man set free,
Death to sin no more,
Now He lives, victory!

All who will believe
God raised Jesus from the grave
Will live forever,
Hallelujah it's Easter Day!

# KING OF GLORY

The King of Glory so precious,
His presence will change your life,
A glance from the Saviour
Will fill you with His light.

He forgives your darkest sin
And heals your deepest wound,
He can love the hardest heart
And a lost soul He will renew.

He will carry you when you're weak
And when you stumble and fall,
He will take your heaviest load
And hear your whisper when you call.

He will come after you when you're lost,
He will lift you when you're down,
He will mend your broken heart,
He will speak without a sound.

The King of Glory took the Cross
To give you eternal life,
A sacrifice for the world,
He came to change the wrong to right.

The King of Glory, Almighty God
One day we will surely meet,
Angels roar for Him in Heaven,
Our eternal Prince of Peace.

## HIS HUMBLE BIRTH…
## WILL BE KNOWN FOREVER…

"The Lord says, "Bethlehem Ephrathah, you are one of the
smallest towns in Judah, but out of you I will bring
a ruler for Israel, whose family line goes back to ancient times."

Micah 5 : 2

# CHRISTMAS IS YOU LORD

Christmas is You Lord,
You came quietly that Holy Night,
Angels rejoiced in garrison
Now You have arrived.

Born humbly in a stable,
A Manger for Your bed,
Swaddling clothes wrapped around You,
By the Star the Magi were led.

The shepherds in the fields
Came to worship You,
The lamb and the calf
Adored You too.

Christmas is You Lord,
God's gift to the world,
You will grow into the Saviour,
Your message You will tell.

You stand for truth and grace,
Mercy is Your Crown,
Peace and love Your message,
In You eternal life is found.

Christmas is You Lord,
We bow on bended knee,
We adore You in the Manger,
The Messiah You'll always be.

# HEAVENLY ANGELS SING OUT

Heavenly angels sing out
To the Shepherds across the fields,
The Saviour is born,
Prophecy now revealed.

In the Manger He lay
Wrapped snuggly and warm,
Adored by the Shepherds
That first Christmas morn.

What joy shone around
The Stable that night,
God's Son born of Mary,
This Holy Night.

Heavenly angels sing out
In wonder and awe,
Hallelujah, Hallelujah,
The Saviour is born!

# IMMANUEL, THE LORD

The perfect gift for everyone,
Christ Jesus, The Lord,
Born in a Manger
That first Christmas morn.

Heavenly Hosts proclaimed
His humble birth,
Their voices rang out
To the Shepherds first.

What joy and wonder
Filled the stable with awe,
The Blessed Mary and Joseph
Adoring God's baby boy.

Sheep and the cattle
Came to worship Him too,
The Lord God Almighty,
Immanuel, they knew.

The perfect gift, Jesus,
Immanuel, Christ the Lord
Arrived this Holy night,
He came for us all.

Immanuel, our Lord,
Perfect in every way,
Glory, glory, glory,
The birth of Christmas Day!

## THE SAVIOUR IS BORN

What joy was theirs
That first Christmas morn,
Wonder in the Stable,
Messiah King, just born!

Their hearts filled with awe
For their Heavenly King,
Saviour and Redeemer,
Eternal life He will bring.

The shepherds, sheep and cattle
Came to worship and adore,
Immanuel, our God
This Holy night is born.

All glory above,
Heavenly angels rejoice,
Christ Jesus in the Manger,
The Saviour is born.

Rejoice, rejoice,
The Saviour is born,
Great glory in Heaven
For Jesus our Lord!

## ALSO BY CLAIRE GROSE

  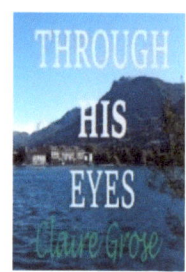

  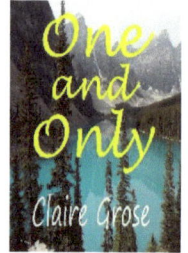

## ABOUT THE AUTHOR

Claire worked as a Government Public Servant in the Lands Department, Adelaide, South Australia until she married and became a mother of two boys.

She later returned to the work force during which time she gained a "Living Hope" Phone Counselling certificate which influenced her need to help others.

Through this and personal experience she found herself inspired by God's love to put pen to paper.

## PHOTO CREDITS

COVER PHOTO:   Sunset, Fleurieu Peninsula taken by Joshua Woskett

Page 2:  Brighton Beach;  S.A. – Claire Grose
Page 12:  Daisy Bush;  S.A. – Lindsay
Page 24:  Duckling Family; Fremont Park  S.A. – Claire Grose
Page 31:  Petunia patch;  S.A. – Claire Grose
Page 39:  African Daisies;  S.A. – Claire Grose
Page 47:  Hastings Point;  N.S.W. – Claire Grose
Page 55:  Blossom Tree;  S.A. – Claire Grose
Page 70:  Ginger Plant;  N.S.W. – Claire Grose
Page 78:  Rose Garden;  S.A. – Jane and Scott
Page 87: Salisbury Uniting Church;  S.A. – Claire Grose
Page 92: Salisbury Uniting Church;  S.A. – Claire Grose
Page 96: Salisbury Uniting Church;  S.A. – Claire Grose

SOLDIERS OF THE LIGHT

www.ingramcontent.com/pod-product-compliance
Lightning Source LLC
Chambersburg PA
CBHW041500010526
44107CB00044B/1512